Airswimming

by Charlotte Jones

WWW.SAMUELFRENCH.CO.UK
WWW.SAMUELFRENCH.COM

Copyright © 2016 by Charlotte Jones
All Rights Reserved

AIRSWIMMING is fully protected under the copyright laws of the British Commonwealth, including Canada, the United States of America, and all other countries of the Copyright Union. All rights, including professional and amateur stage productions, recitation, lecturing, public reading, motion picture, radio broadcasting, television and the rights of translation into foreign languages are strictly reserved.

ISBN 978-0-573-03025-3

www.samuelfrench.co.uk

www.samuelfrench.com

FOR AMATEUR PRODUCTION ENQUIRIES

UNITED KINGDOM AND WORLD EXCLUDING NORTH AMERICA
plays@SamuelFrench-London.co.uk
020 7255 4302/01

UNITED STATES AND CANADA
info@SamuelFrench.com
1-866-598-8449

Each title is subject to availability from Samuel French, depending upon country of performance.

CAUTION: Professional and amateur producers are hereby warned that AIRSWIMMING is subject to a licensing fee. Publication of this play does not imply availability for performance. Both amateurs and professionals considering a production are strongly advised to apply to the appropriate agent before starting rehearsals, advertising, or booking a theatre. A licensing fee must be paid whether the title is presented for charity or gain and whether or not admission is charged.

The professional rights in this play are controlled by United Agents LLP, 12-26 Lexington Street, London, W1F OLE.

No one shall make any changes in this title for the purpose of production. No part of this book may be reproduced, stored in a retrieval system, or transmitted in any form, by any means, now known or yet to be invented, including mechanical, electronic, photocopying, recording, videotaping, or otherwise, without the prior written permission of the publisher. No one shall upload this title, or part of this title, to any social media websites.

The right of Charlotte Jones to be identified as author of this work has been asserted in accordance with Section 77 of the Copyright, Designs and Patents Act 1988.

Author's note

Airswimming is a comedy about despair. It was inspired by the various true stories of women who were placed in mental institutions in the 1920s because they had given birth to illegitimate children, or for other spurious reasons such as they were deaf, lesbian or merely "atypical". Some of these women were not released until the 1970s when a lot of the Victorian mental institutions closed down as the great age of pharmacology had dawned. It is a meditation on stasis, on being stuck in a hopeless situation and the salvation that is to be found only in friendship.

The dance and song elements are crucial to the sense of joy that the play can bring in performance. DORA and PERSEPHONE find each other and remain essentially free even though they are incarcerated because of the pleasure and solace they find in each other's company. As Viktor Frankl wrote so movingly in his book *Man's Search for Meaning*: "Everything can be taken from a man but one thing: the last of the human freedoms – to choose one's attitude in any given set of circumstances, to choose one's own way." DORA and PERSEPHONE manage to save each other and transform into DORPH and PORPH in order to survive.

Charlotte Jones

USE OF COPYRIGHT MUSIC

A licence issued by Samuel French Ltd to perform this play does not include permission to use any music specified in this copy. Where the place of performance is already licensed by the PERFORMING RIGHT SOCIETY a return of the music used must be made to them. If the place of performance is not so licensed then application should be made to the Performing Right Society, 29 Berners Street, London W1T 3AB. Before your performance please make sure you are adhering to the UK copyright laws.

A separate and additional licence from
PHONOGRAPHIC PERFORMANCES LTD, 1 Upper James Street, London W1R 3HG is needed whenever commercial recordings are used.

Airswimming was first presented by Sweet Desserts Theatre Company at the Battersea Arts Centre, London, on 31 January 1997. The cast was as follows:

Persephone / Porph **Rosie Cavaliero**

Dora / Dorph **Charlotte Jones**

Director **Anna Mackmin**

Designer **Kirsty Twaddle**

Lighting **Sue Baynton**

Choreography **Scarlett Mackmin**

Character list

DORA/ DORPH – female, darker in tone, comical.

PERSEPHONE/ PORPH – female, lighter in tone, comical.

There are options in the playing of the two characters. Both women age by fifty years and are traditionally played by actresses in their twenties – their age at the beginning of the play as DORA and PERSEPHONE. However they could equally be played by actresses in their 70s – the age they are as DORPH and PORPH. In fact I see no reason why they couldn't be played by actresses of any age. There is also the option that the cast could expand to four actresses so that there is no doubling.

Scene One

Lights up.

An institutionalised interior. Drab and hostile. Possibly tiled like a bathroom or swimming pool.

A tin bath. And a staircase or possibly a stepladder. A box.

A picture of a saint (Saint Dymphna) on the back wall.

DORA *is polishing vigorously, whistling.* **PERSEPHONE** *enters with cloth in hand, looking bewildered.*

DORA It's like the trenches.

PERSEPHONE Trenches?

DORA Yes, its like being in the trenches.

PERSEPHONE What?

DORA <u>Here</u>. It's like being in the trenches here.

PERSEPHONE Oh.

DORA You're the new girl.

PERSEPHONE What? I don't know, yes.

DORA How's your elbow.?

PERSEPHONE I beg your pardon.

DORA Elbow?

PERSEPHONE Fine thank you.

DORA Good, here we need strong elbows. We have no need of a nicely turned ankle, an elegant wrist, a swan-like neck. No, here you need damn good elbows.

PERSEPHONE I see.

1

DORA Lots of elbow grease.

PERSEPHONE Yes.

DORA Bath. You're supposed to clean the bath. Get to it then. At the double.

PERSEPHONE Sorry.

DORA Come on, long bold strokes. We've got to do the floor, the stairs and the bath before four. Trouble is, there's never any proper training here. Wouldn't let it happen in my regiment. Don't like sloppy work.

PERSEPHONE I can't, I mean I never have. I don't know how to.

DORA That's neither here nor there.

PERSEPHONE *(on the verge of breakdown)* I'm very tired. *(pause)*

DORA Ever heard of Catalina de Frangipani?

PERSEPHONE No, no I haven't.

DORA Didn't think so. In 1657 Catalina was training to be a nun, first order of the Weeping Magdalenas. On the night before she was due to take her vows, she escaped the convent, scaling a twenty-foot-high wall. Incidentally she was only four-foot seven. Yes she scaled that mountainous wall and ran away and joined the army. Fought for the Spanish all over South America. She made a lousy Weeping Magdalena you see, but a formidable soldier.

PERSEPHONE I'm sorry?

DORA Apparently she survived on 27 minutes sleep every night. Lived till she was ninety.

PERSEPHONE Oh.

DORA Being tired did not enter into it.

PERSEPHONE No.

> **PERSEPHONE** *starts to clean. Stops.*

It's just that I'm not quite sure where I am. Or why I'm here.

DORA They didn't brief you?

PERSEPHONE What? No. Nobody's told me a thing.

DORA Negative. Well the duty falls to me. You are now an honorary Dymphonian.

PERSEPHONE What?

DORA The new girl. A freshman. A private of course. But you must prepare yourself for a long haul.

PERSEPHONE I'm sorry I don't...

DORA St. Dymphna's Hospital for the Criminally Insane.

PERSEPHONE I'm in hospital?

DORA For the Criminally Insane, yes. St Dymphna's – there she is. *(she gestures towards picture)*

I am Dora Kitson and we are now on polishing duty. The year is, correct me if I'm wrong, which incidentally I never am, 1924. All present and correct. I've been here since 1922. Yes, stationed here July 4th – American Independence Day – funny that. The irony is not lost on me, believe you me. I shall be your superior officer for a while, but don't worry, I'm not one to pull rank. We do this polishing duty for one hour each day. The rest of the time we shuffle and look crazed. They prefer it that way. This is probably the only time we get to talk as they need two of us to do it. They generally leave us alone. The last one was too feeble to do it any longer. To tell you the truth she wasn't up to much. Deaf mute you see. Nice enough soul but talk about blood out of a stone. I'd have given her compassionate leave straight off. No, I need someone with their wits about them. Beleaguered lot here you see. They prefer them with at least one of their faculties missing. Have you got all your faculties, Miss – sorry what did you say your name was? Mm?...You look all right. But then you never can tell. Although usually they've lost it in the eye department. But you can begin to lose it you see when there's no-one to talk to – you know, discuss tactics that sort of thing. I've been there, oh yes I have. Which is why I'm rather pinning my hopes on you Miss...what did you say your name was? ...Hoping you're a bit of a wit and raconteur. Liven up the barracks. Well all this waiting you see. Never know when the battle might commence. But you look all right. Good soldier material... Well at least you can speak, not like the last one... you can speak can't you?

PERSEPHONE There's been a mistake.

DORA Ah yes, a fine soprano lurking in there.

PERSEPHONE There's been a terrible mistake.

DORA Very probably. There are always mistakes. But they are seldom rectified.

PERSEPHONE I must contact my father.

DORA No contact with the outside world I'm afraid. But I'm thrilled you're here. I've waited two years for you.

PERSEPHONE You don't understand. I must get a message through to my father. I absolutely must. I have to speak to someone in authority. Can you call them for me?

DORA It won't do you any good. It's better not to make a fuss. I've tried it and I know. Damn nearly court-marshalled I was.

PERSEPHONE Please, you're not listening to me. Please, please I need to speak to my father. Please help me.

DORA All right, there there. Deep breaths and all that. Who brought you here?

PERSEPHONE Well Daddy but…

DORA Your father brought you here.

PERSEPHONE Well Daddy called the doctor you see. I was just at home. In the nursery. Minding my own business. And this doctor came. A nasty, nasty man. He asked me all sorts of impossible questions. I couldn't answer them. I'm rotten with questions you see. I'm not very bright, Daddy says. And I just couldn't answer them, try as I might. And then they restrained me you see. I was jolly upset. All the questions you see. Mind you I put up a fight. Oh yes I did. And Daddy called me a witch. He called me a witch. Then he brought me here. To convalesce, he said. It all happened so quickly you see.

DORA Yes we must learn to be on our guard at all times.

PERSEPHONE Well, I suppose it's only for a short time. I have been unwell. To convalesce, he said.

DORA That's it. That's the spirit. We might as well finish this now.

PERSEPHONE Sorry.

DORA Yes. It's all right. You find ways of getting through it. You won't think so at first. But you will.

PERSEPHONE I'm only here for a short time. I just didn't realize… till I'm better. Just till I'm better.

DORA Absolutely. Would you mind getting some water? Round the corner to the right.

PERSEPHONE Yes, very well. Sorry.

PERSEPHONE exits. End of Scene One.

We are suddenly in a new reality. Lights change. It is brighter, less hostile.

PERSEPHONE re-enters but she is now PORPH, wearing a bad Doris Day wig.

6   AIRSWIMMING

Scene Two

PORPH Dorph, Dorph. Oh my God. You've got to help me. Please Dorph.

DORPH Porph, calm down, what is it? *Slowly. Take deep breaths.*

PORPH Oh Dorph. I've never been so scared. This big dastardly man came up. You know with a big black moustache. And a very false smile. And unnaturally white teeth.

DORPH Do we have to go through this again Porph?

PORPH Yes, yes. I was very scared. He asked me lots of questions. And I couldn't answer them. So he chased me. He chased me here and there and over there and under there...

DORPH Yes, all right. What questions? Let's go through this. Tell me. What questions did he ask you?

PORPH I don't know. I'm not sure.

DORPH Of course you know, come on Porph.

PORPH I don't remember – impossible questions.

DORPH Like what?

PORPH I don't know.

DORPH I'm not listening any more Porph.

PORPH No, no Dorph. Very hard questions. The hardest type of questions, Sport and Leisure questions.

DORPH Sport and Leisure questions?

PORPH Yes.

DORPH That's new. Like what?

PORPH Like, "In which sport did Betty Wilson make headlines during the 1950s?" Very hard questions. Especially for a girl Dorph.

DORPH Yes.

PORPH And then he chased me.

DORPH Cricket.

PORPH What?

DORPH Betty Wilson was a cricketer. Fast bowler. Famous for her bouncers.

PORPH Yes all right.

DORPH Am I right?

PORPH I don't know.

DORPH I think I am.

PORPH Anyway, the point is he chased me all over the place and I was screaming and screaming and here's the really weird thing Dorph; no sound would come out of my mouth. And then he tied me to a tree. And I couldn't breathe. And nobody could hear me. You couldn't hear me could you Dorph?

DORPH No Porph.

PORPH And I thought I was going to die. And I was frantic and I was crying, and I was tearing my hair out.

DORPH I thought you were tied up.

PORPH I was… I was but I could just reach my hair. It was slightly longer then.

DORPH And then what happened?

PORPH I managed to get free.

DORPH That was lucky.

PORPH Yes but I'm completely exhausted.

Pause.

DORPH There was no man was there Porph?

PORPH No Dorph.

DORPH And he – that man that didn't exist, he didn't ask you any questions did he? And if he had asked you questions you might have been able to answer them mightn't you? They might have been easy questions mightn't they? And then he didn't chase you and tie you to a tree because, besides that he didn't exist, there are no trees around here, and he didn't have any rope and you didn't need to scream for help and if you had I would have heard you wouldn't I because, besides that there is nothing wrong with your voice-box, I have exceptionally good hearing and anyway there was no man, with or without a moustache and you have been safe here with me all morning, so you're not in any danger are you Porph?

PORPH No Dorph… Well I'm glad we cleared that one up.

DORPH Good.

PORPH But Dorph, what if I was in critical danger?

DORPH I'm losing my patience with you.

PORPH What if I accidentally fell into a persistent vegetative state?

DORPH I might find it difficult to tell Porph.

PORPH Dorph! What if I was struck by a herd of marauding beasts and I didn't have clean knickers on and then I got sucked into a swamp against my will and then I became a Christian against my better nature and I was forced to wear Lycra and then I lost my vitals and in the meantime my cortex was crumbling and I didn't know the way home?

DORPH You really are a terrible worrier Porph. The worst case scenario doesn't always happen. You mustn't torment yourself. You're here with me and nothing and nobody else matters.

PORPH Thank you Dorph. You help me get through things. I didn't think you could but you do.

DORPH Good.

PORPH Have you noticed? I'm wearing it.

DORPH What?

PORPH My new Doris Day wig.

DORPH Ah, so I see.

PORPH Do you know what?

DORPH What?

PORPH I think it's time for a song in my new Doris Day wig.

DORPH I've got to do some reading Porph.

PORPH Only a quiet one. A lullaby. Doris's million-dollar hit from *The Man Who Knew Too Much*, co-starring James Stewart. Are you ready Dorph?

She sings eight lines from Que Sera Sera "Whatever Will Be, Will Be".

PORPH *sighs.*

What a truly beautiful song Dorph.

DORPH I think it is unrivalled in the beauty stakes Porph.

PORPH And very deep don't you think? I find it oddly comforting, you know. When I'm a little bit down in the dumps. Or under the weather, I just think to myself "Que Sera Sera" and I really genuinely feel a whole lot better.

DORPH Doris Day never skimps on the truth does she Porph? She tells it like it is.

PORPH Thank you for that Dorph... What are you reading?

DORPH A book of spells.

PORPH What's it like being a sister of Wicca Dorph?

DORPH What?

PORPH You know the "W" word... *(she whispers)* Witch.

DORPH Oh you know Porph. It has its ups and downs. You're your own boss. You're not cooped up in an office. But there's not much security. No long-term pension plan; and there's always the risk that your neighbours will duck you in the village pond or burn you to death.

PORPH Yes there is that. Why do people do such terrible things to other people?

DORPH Witches are evil Porph. They're destructive. They cut off male members and eat them for breakfast. They're sexually crazed.

PORPH Well you're not that are you Dorph. You never get it at all.

DORPH I'm not a witch Porph.

PORPH But you said –

DORPH I said sometimes I felt like a witch. It's very different Porph. I just don't trust people any more. It's better if we keep ourselves to ourselves.

PORPH You know Doris has lost complete faith in people now. That's why she founded the Doris Day Pet Foundation. She's dedicated her life to animals now.

DORPH That woman really is a saint isn't she Porph? Let's hope she gets recognised very soon for what she's done for mankind.

PORPH That day is coming very soon Dorph.

DORPH Good. Time for bed. Don't forget to say your prayers.

PORPH Dear Lord; God bless Doris Day and the Doris Day Pet Foundation and let Doris get the Nobel Prize for...Literature or something soon and God bless Porph and Dorph and keep us safe and together forever. Amen.

DORPH Good girl. Go to sleep. I've got some tidying to do.

Lights change.

Scene Three

DORA *and* **PERSEPHONE** *are cleaning, but* **PERSEPHONE** *in a very half-hearted way.*

DORA Good morning. It could be worse we could be on laundry duty.

PERSEPHONE *ignores her.*

Yes, they've got quite a system going there. *(pause)*

The delirious wash, the imbeciles carry the linen to dry, the melancholy iron it and the monomaniacs fold it and put it away. And we have to sleep on those sheets. No wonder we all have nightmares. Yes, it's a shame. After all even nutters need their beauty sleep, what do you think?

PERSEPHONE What are you?

DORA I'm sorry?

PERSEPHONE What's wrong with you?

DORA Nothing.

PERSEPHONE Why are you here then?

DORA Why are you here?

Silence.

It's hard at first, I know. But you have to keep focussed. Like Joan of Arc. Incarceration didn't get her down. She took it like a man. Refused to wear frocks. Had a short crop. They thought it was deviancy. I try to be deviant whenever I can. *Vive la deviance.*

PERSEPHONE Are you mad?

DORA I beg your pardon?

PERSEPHONE Criminally insane. Well I assume you are. You seem to be.

DORA Certainly not. I resent the suggestion. Criminally insane. The idea of it! Unless a predilection for Spanish cigars counts.

PERSEPHONE What?

DORA That's what first got them alerted to me. To my deviancy. I enjoyed the odd smoke. Shouldn't have done it. It's not de rigeur. But whether it's criminally insane. That's a different matter. What do you think, Miss – ummm?

PERSEPHONE About what?

DORA Smoking cigars.

PERSEPHONE I think it's perfectly foul. I can't believe anyone in their right mind would want to.

DORA Ah typical woman. There are pleasures in this world that you know nothing of.

PERSEPHONE Well I'm rather glad. Life isn't supposed to be all pleasure.

DORA Ah indeed you are so right, Miss – umm. In fact you have inadvertently hit upon our little motto here. What is the Latin now? *Vitam sine pleasurae* or some such. Life without joy. We Dymphonians live by that. Not that we feel sorry for ourselves, oh no. They also serve who only sit and polish. I can see you're going to fit in here, Miss Ummm –

PERSEPHONE I'm not here for long.

DORA Oh.

PERSEPHONE No. I'll be leaving any day now. They're coming back to get me you see. So there's no point getting your hopes up about me. I'll be leaving you very soon.

DORA Ah, what a shame.

PERSEPHONE Yes, isn't it. But it can't be helped I'm afraid. I'm coming out very soon you see. Before the King. My parents are arranging a huge party at the Dorchester. I'll be dressed in white satin from head to toe. So I can't possibly miss it. It will be the most important day of my life. Apart from my wedding day. So I have to be there. In the meantime I just have to sit tight. Get strong. This is just my convalescence home – I'd have preferred Geneva or somewhere Swiss. I can't understand why they chose here. But ours is not to reason why, what will be, will be, Mummy always says.

DORA Does she now?

PERSEPHONE Yes, like one time I wanted this hat. It was huge and pink with big squashy flowers all over it and I thought it was the most beautiful hat in the world but looking back on it it was rather vulgar but at the time it would have made me very happy but Daddy said I couldn't and I was so vexed I cried and cried and all Mummy said was, "Ours is not to reason why, Persephone Baker, what will be, will be." Which I found oddly comforting at the time although it would have been better to have the hat I think, in fact, looking back on it it wasn't comforting at all and I should have had the hat even if I never wore it. I said to Reggie – *(looks at* **DORA***)* – well it doesn't matter. I didn't get the hat and now I'm here we're not allowed to have pretty hats so maybe it's just as well. Although I shall need one for my coming out. So I'll just sit tight. But don't get it into your head that I'm staying. Because I'm not. I expect they're coming any day now. At the end of the week probably. A fortnight at the most... *(she trails off)*

Pause.

DORA Persephone Baker.

PERSEPHONE What?

DORA Your name.

PERSEPHONE What about it?

DORA Nothing. I just didn't know it. You hadn't told me. I'm very pleased to make your acquaintance, Miss Baker.

PERSEPHONE Yes. Well. It won't be for long.

DORA No clearly. We'd better get down to this then. Sharpish. Before you get whisked away.

PERSEPHONE Yes, we'd better.

DORA Yes like Persephone to the Underworld, Hades will return and take you thither.

PERSEPHONE I beg your pardon?

DORA The Greek myth, you know... Well we'd better get on with this.

PERSEPHONE Oh. Yes.

DORA And by the way, Miss Baker you have a lovely voice. Music to my ears.

PERSEPHONE Oh right. Thank you.

DORA Yes. Feel free to break into song at any time.

Scene Four

> **PORPH** *goes to the box and gets out her wig and puts it on.*
> **DORPH** *gets a book out and starts to read.*

PORPH *(sings five lines from* Everybody Loves A Lover*)*

DORPH Guess I might be trying to read, Pollyanna.

PORPH You're always reading.

DORPH Yes so be quiet.

PORPH What are you reading?

DORPH You won't be interested.

PORPH Yes I will. I like books and I have a wide range of hobbies and interests.

DORPH Trepanning.

PORPH What?

DORPH It's about trepanning.

PORPH That's nice.

DORPH Yes.

PORPH What is it?

DORPH Trepanning?

PORPH Yes.

DORPH It's drilling two small holes in your skull, about here and here.

PORPH Why?

DORPH To make you feel happier.

PORPH Happier?

DORPH Yes

PORPH Are you sure?

DORPH Yes.

PORPH It doesn't sound much fun to me.

DORPH Well you don't need to do it.

PORPH Oh Dorph are you unhappy again?

DORPH What could I possibly be unhappy about?

PORPH I wish I could help you.

DORPH You don't have to stay with me. You can go at any time.

PORPH Shush now Dorph. You know Bob Hope once said about Doris, that she had the rare quality of making people feel good just by walking on stage.

DORPH If only she were here now Porph.

PORPH Yes, but I think that in this wig there is a striking similarity between myself and Doris. Let's see if I can do it. Hold on Dorph.

> **PORPH** *walks off stage and walks back on a la Doris.*

Feel any better Dorph?

DORPH That was uncanny Porph.

PORPH Did I have that rare quality of making you feel good just by walking on stage?

DORPH You do have a rare quality Porph.

PORPH Shall I do it again?

DORPH I think I've had my fill.

PORPH So you feel better.

DORPH It has affected me greatly.

PORPH I was imbued, just for that second, with the spirit of Doris I think. I can feel her presence even now Dorph. Can you?

DORPH Porph when I'm with you I can truthfully say that I can't get Doris Day out of my head. I shut my eyes and she is there, I close my ears and I still hear her, even in sleep I cannot quite rid myself of the image of this woman who, after all, only made a handful of films almost four decades ago.

PORPH You are very lucky Dorph. It's like she's your spiritual guide. You're very very lucky.

DORPH Que sera sera.

PORPH Now put away that book. Neither I nor Doris will hear anymore of you bedpanning yourself.

DORPH Trepanning.

PORPH Yes all right. Drilling holes in your head. I've never heard the like. Now I've got a surprise for you.

She collects a present from the box.

Here.

DORPH What is it?

PORPH Well open it.

DORPH Is this what I think it is? Because really its not a problem Porph.

PORPH Open it!

She opens it.

DORPH What is it?

PORPH Its a Moulinex hand whisk.

DORPH What do I want with this?

PORPH It's battery operated.

DORPH Yes?

PORPH It's a brilliant labour-saving device.

DORPH It's an instrument of evil.

PORPH Oh Dorph. You can do all sorts with it.

DORPH Like what?

PORPH Stir and whisk and whoosh things up in a bowl. Ingredients. Whirr. In a bowl.

DORPH I don't need this. I never bake. You know I never bake. I've made a point of never baking. Take it back, Porph.

PORPH But it's my present to you. I like it. It's made by Moulinex. Please can we keep it?

DORPH Oh all right.

PORPH Can I have a cat as well?

DORPH Porph I've told you, no. You can keep the whisk but a cat is out of the question.

PORPH Oh all right.

DORPH Don't sulk. It's time for bed.

PORPH Do you feel any better Dorph?

DORPH Yes thank you. I'm fine.

PORPH You worry about what other people say about you don't you?

DORPH No, no, come on I'm tired.

PORPH Can I sing to you?

DORPH If you like.

PORPH Can it be Doris.

DORPH Of course. It's always Doris Porph.

PORPH What shall it be. I know –

She sings seven lines from Make Someone Happy.

DORPH That's nice Porph.

PORPH You sleep Dorphy.

PORPH *collects the whisk quietly, still singing – then looks troubled.*

Dorph, are you asleep?

DORPH Yes.

PORPH I need to ask you something very urgently.

DORPH What?

PORPH Was Doris Day a virgin?

DORPH What?

PORPH It's all right, you can tell me.

DORPH She wasn't to begin with, but then she became one.

PORPH Like me.

DORPH Yes Porph, like you.

PORPH That's good. Goodnight Dorph.

She settles down to sleep immediately. **DORPH** *looks troubled.*

DORPH Goodnight.

Scene Five

DORA Do you want to do the bath or the stairs?

PERSEPHONE I think you've mistaken me for someone who gives a damn.

DORA I'll do the stairs then.

Silence.

The folks didn't show?

Silence.

So how are you settling in then, Miss Baker? Perfectly comfortable are we? It's not the Dorchester is it? Although most of our guests stay for much longer. It's the camaraderie I think. Have you met some of the others? Oh it's just like a barracks here, we all muck in, help each other. Although insolence to our superior officers does not go unnoticed. But we have fun, oh yes we do. There's even talk of a ball, you know. Our own big coming out party. Except none of us will be. Coming out, that is. More of a staying in ball. But we know how to have a good time. Agnes is always good value. Have you met her? Mad as a snake and horny as a ram – one tooth and no hair to speak of. She'd make rather a good gun dog, come to think of it. Little terrier, you see. Yes some of them are really wild. Some of them are just children. Lots of cripples... Drawn from all walks of life. No we don't stand on ceremony here. I wonder where you'll fit in, Miss Baker.

PERSEPHONE I'm a moral imbecile.

DORA What?

PERSEPHONE It says so in my notes. I had to see the doctor. He left me alone and I read them. I'm a moral imbecile. Do you know what that is? Reggie would know I'm sure of it. Anyway they're not coming to get me, are they? That's clear enough even to a moral imbecile.

DORA I'm sorry.

PERSEPHONE No you're not. Anyway I'd better get down to it. I'd like to finish the stairs since I always get the bath.

DORA Feel free.

PERSEPHONE Yes and I'd like to point out here and now that I'm afraid I don't like you. You don't have any manners, you talk too much and you seem to think you're a man when clearly you're a girl. In fact you remind me of my Great Aunt Martha. I hated going to see her when I was little because she barked like a dog and stank like one too. She was jilted not unsurprisingly. Nobody liked her. I'm sure she would have fitted in very well here. Anyway, Miss Kitson, fate has dealt us a cruel blow in putting us together but Reggie would have told me to be brave and put up with it. So put up with it I shall.

DORA Who's Reggie?

PERSEPHONE It's none of your business.

Silence.

DORA People don't warm to me, it's a funny thing. Even the last one. The deaf mute. She didn't actually say anything but the way she would occasionally spit at me gave her away you see… Yes. So. Your Great Aunt Martha. Reminds me of Hannah Snell, you know. She was jilted in 1745. I'm remarkable with dates, had you noticed? Anyway yes, she was jilted but she didn't go to seed, oh no. She joined the navy. Another top drawer soldier. She received 12 wounds at the British Naval assault on Pondicherry in 1748. Even extracted a ball from her own groin to prevent discovery of her sex. Just think of it! Perhaps that's what old Martha should have done. The naval bit not the groin bit.

PERSEPHONE I'm really not interested.

Pause.

DORA It's certainly not necessary that we like each other.

PERSEPHONE Good.

DORA Although it might be nice. And I have a plan that might involve you.

PERSEPHONE *(reluctantly)* What?

DORA Keep it under your hat.

PERSEPHONE I haven't got a hat.

DORA No of course. Well would you like to hear it?

PERSEPHONE If you really must.

DORA *(confidentially)* Code name of operation: GOD.

PERSEPHONE GOD?

DORA Get out of Dymphna. Date of operation, any day now.

PERSEPHONE Great.

DORA Time of operation: sixteen hundred hours.

PERSEPHONE Couldn't you wait till after tea?

DORA Short term and long term aim of operation: to get out of Dymphna.

PERSEPHONE God help us, you're talking about escaping. And how exactly are you going to escape?

DORA Well, I'm still working that one through. Still a bit tied up on the logistics. But I thought two heads would be better than one.

PERSEPHONE Miss Kitson, look around you. People die before they get out of here. And if we did get out, who would have us? We have no family. We have no money. We have no hope.

Silence.

DORA At times like these I think of Judith, of her courage. Flirted with the attacking General, drank him under the table and then whacked off his head and stuck it in a picnic basket.

PERSEPHONE Please. Please. You're not helping me.

DORA I'd like to be able to help you.

PERSEPHONE Well you can't. Nobody can. I just have to put up with it. What will be, will be. I think it would be very much better if we spent this hour in silence, don't you?

Pause.

DORA I'm sorry if I'm annoying you.

Pause.

PERSEPHONE It's not your fault.

> **PERSEPHONE** *goes to clean the picture of St Dymphna.*

She's got a lot to answer for.

DORA What? Ah the venerable Dymphna.

PERSEPHONE Who was she anyway?

DORA Born 1034. Woman of extraordinary beauty. Unfortunately her father thought so too. He repeatedly forced himself on her until she bore his child which he murdered and she starved herself to death. Now she's our patron saint. Patron saint of moral imbeciles.

PERSEPHONE Why do people do such terrible things to other people?

DORA There are those who would say she was on a losing wicket to begin with. With a name like Dymphna.

PERSEPHONE It is a peculiar name.

DORA Terrible name. Dymphna. With a name like that what else could she be but patron saint of the mentally unbalanced?

PERSEPHONE Well she'd better start pulling her finger out because I'm a moral imbecile. And I'm in bloody trouble.

Scene Six

PORPH Good morning Doris.

DORPH *reads.*

Sings three lines from Teacher's Pet.

DORPH Are you going to give me trouble today?

PORPH *(sings a further three lines from* Teacher's Pet.*)*

DORPH I know you.

PORPH I thought maybe we might go swimming later, Dorph. *(sings a further three lines from* Teacher's Pet.*)*

DORPH No.

PORPH Oh, Dorph!

DORPH No.

PORPH But I love swimming.

DORPH I told you it's better if we stay here. Anyway the baths are filthy. You'll get verrucas.

PORPH I like verrucas.

DORPH Porph!

PORPH Can I have a cat then?

DORPH Look, we'll go swimming later.

PORPH Really?

DORPH Yes. But a different kind of swimming. Much less hazardous.

PORPH Sometimes I am weighed down by the boredom of my life.

DORPH How about a story?

PORPH Yes!

DORPH Good girl. Now. Let's see. Our story today is of Persephone.

PORPH Persephone.

DORPH Yes. Persephone lived with her mother, Demeter.

PORPH Demeter.

DORPH And her two sisters, Artemis –

PORPH Artemis.

DORPH And Athene –

PORPH Athene.

DORPH Yes thank you Porph you don't have to repeat all the names.

PORPH Sorry.

DORPH And Persephone was very beautiful with hair like spun gold. And she lived happily with her mother and sisters.

PORPH Like us?

DORPH Yes like us Porph. Until one day –

PORPH Oh no!

DORPH What?

PORPH Something bad, I know.

DORPH A man came. His name was Hades.

PORPH A big ugly dark hairy Turk of a man.

DORPH Yes all right, Porph. Who's telling this story?

PORPH Sorry, Dorph.

DORPH And he saw Persephone with her hair like spun gold and he wanted her. Like he'd never wanted anything else before.

PORPH Like I want a cat?

DORPH Porph!

PORPH Sorry, Dorph.

DORPH So he stole her away. And took her to the Underworld. Now Demeter loved her daughter so much that she lost her marbles.

PORPH I lost my marbles once.

DORPH Yes, well she wanted her daughter back so much that she decided to use the only power she had to bring her back.

PORPH She cut off his member.

DORPH No she withered the crops. She turned summer into winter.

PORPH I bet you could do that, Dorph. And what did the hairy bloke do?

DORPH Well the two of them struck a bargain. They decided to share her. Demeter had Persephone for the summer months and Hades had her for the winter.

PORPH *(appalled)* And what did Persephone say?

DORPH The story doesn't tell us what she said, Porph.

PORPH Couldn't she speak?

DORPH Oh yes I think she had a lovely voice.

PORPH Then why didn't she stop them?

DORPH Perhaps they didn't listen to her.

PORPH Frankly I am appalled at the outcome for poor Persephone. I feel very sorry for her, Dorph.

DORPH Yes, well.

PORPH Someone ought to help the poor girl out.

DORPH It's all right, Porph.

PORPH No, but I mean –

DORPH No, it's all right, Porph. Because you see in the film version, Persephone is played by Doris Day.

PORPH *(relieved)* Oh I see and she manages to win them all over with her sweet girl-next-door image, natural good looks and extraordinary singing voice.

DORPH Exactly.

PORPH Well that's a relief. We love Doris, don't we Dorph.

DORPH She made happy pictures about happy people, Porph.

PORPH And when she cried, she cried funny... How do you do that, Dorph?

DORPH Only Doris knows.

PORPH I don't think I'd like it if everybody laughed at me when I cried.

DORPH No well, that's why Doris Day is a major motion picture star and you're just Porph.

PORPH Yes I see, Dorph.

DORPH Now come on for your swimming lesson.

PORPH Where are we swimming, Dorph?

DORPH We're going to swim through the air, Porph.

PORPH Do you know, Dorph, I feel like Calamity Jane when I'm with you.

DORPH Is that good?

PORPH *(impersonates Doris Day)* Why of course it is, yes, siree, you give me the finest time in Chicagee. Better even than Wild Bill Hickok.

DORPH Come on then, Calam, get the goggles.

They get goggles, swim caps and nose clips out of the box. They put them on.

I think you might have to lose the wig, Porph.

PORPH No, no Dorph. See I've got my swimcap on.

DORPH Are you ready, Porph?

PORPH Let's get cracking.

DORPH Right.

Music. Doris Day Fly Me To The Moon

Let's go.

They hold hands and do synchronised air-swimming routine.

At the end of the routine they put their things away and revert to St Dymphna's.

Scene Seven

PERSEPHONE Stairs.

DORA Bath.

Pause.

PERSEPHONE Sometimes Miss Kitson, I imagine I'm in a film. I'm the heroine naturally.

DORA Naturally.

PERSEPHONE And one of those dastardly men comes up. You know the sort – with mad eyes and fierce black moustaches. And anyway he's tied me to the lamp post or even better the railway tracks. And the train is coming. Well of course I'm quite frantic. I'm screaming for all I'm worth.

DORA I expect you're a dab hand at screaming.

PERSEPHONE Yes, well I look extremely beautiful even though I'm dishevelled. I'm very worried but then part of me knows that I'll be saved in the end.

DORA Your hero.

PERSEPHONE Exactly. My hero. But of course he doesn't come until the very last moment. It would ruin it all if he arrived too early. All hope must be lost. I must be on the absolute brink of disaster.

DORA Of course.

PERSEPHONE He snatches me from the jaws of death. Do you ever have fantasies like that?

DORA Not exactly like that, no.

PERSEPHONE *(persisting)* But say you did. If someone was going to snatch you from the jaws of death, who would it be?

DORA Well, I suppose it would have to be Maria Bochkareva.

PERSEPHONE I don't think I want to know.

DORA Yes, remarkable woman. Russian Bolshevik soldier. Founded an all-woman crack corps of 2000 high-grade volunteers. Called them the "Women's Battalion of Death".

PERSEPHONE Really.

DORA Yes I quite fancy being snatched from the jaws of death by 2000 Bolshevick women with rifles.

PERSEPHONE *looks at her incredulously. Pause.*

PERSEPHONE Anyway the point is I suppose that I want someone to snatch me from the jaws of all this. I know I shouldn't but I can't help myself.

DORA Who would it be?

PERSEPHONE Reggie. You know I can see him striding down those stairs to sweep me off my feet.

DORA I'd have to have them widened.

PERSEPHONE What?

DORA The stairs... If Maria Bochkareva and her "Women's Battalion of Death" were going to save me.

PERSEPHONE Yes, well there's no point thinking about it, is there?

DORA *returns to her cleaning but notices that* **PERSEPHONE** *is lost in thought.*

DORA Where did you meet him?

PERSEPHONE You're not really interested.

DORA Why not? It might make you feel better. Get it off your chest and all that.

PERSEPHONE I doubt it.

DORA Suit yourself.

PERSEPHONE At a friend's 21st birthday party. I met him at a friend's 21st. I fell in love with him at first sight.

Pause.

He was 30 years older than me. He had a wife. He had two children. He was an acquaintance of my father's. Madness, I know. There was never any question of ever breaking anything up. Although his relationship with his wife was very, very patchy.

DORA I see.

PERSEPHONE He asked me to dance. I turned bright beetroot. I was quivering all over. We got up. On the dance floor I was electrified from head to foot. Afterwards he crumpled and I crumpled. I'd never known a man cry and he blubbed like a schoolboy. He was crying for me, which was most gratifying. He was bonkers about me. And I absolutely adored this man. *(pause)*

Haven't you ever felt anything like that for a man, Miss Kitson?

DORA Well, I suppose I admire a man in a uniform. But then again it's more the uniform than the man I think.

PERSEPHONE Oh how could I have expected you to understand, you of all people.

DORA Sorry.

PERSEPHONE No, you're bloody not. Oh what have I ever done to deserve you. I don't think I can bear this much longer. *(pause)* Never say never, Mummy always said. But don't you see that here you can always say never. I'll never see Reggie again, never kiss him and hold him. I'll never see my family, never come out, never get married, never wear fine dresses, never buy hats. The weight of it all is killing me. I'll never dance again, for God's sake. I'll never dance. And I'm such a fine dancer. The best, Reggie said. I can't bear it. Never to get up and dance. Simply dance. The only certainty in my life is you. An unhinged cigar smoking monomaniac transsexual. I must have done something really terrible. Beyond terrible.

Pause.

DORA I'll dance with you.

PERSEPHONE *(horrified)* What?

DORA I'll dance with you.

PERSEPHONE YOU!

DORA Why not? I don't see Reggie anywhere. And I want to help in some small way. It's worse for you because you're a lady. And there's nothing to say we can't dance. Well actually I can't dance. But I'm willing to give it a go. You could teach me something simple. Then I could be the man. And lead. It might make us feel better. A bit of exercise. A bit of fun.

PERSEPHONE NO! I mean no thank you, Miss Kitson, it's very kind of you. But I don't think it's a very good idea. I mean you're not trying to… I mean, you don't find me –

DORA Good God, no. Nothing like that. I'm sorry. Stupid idea. Forget I spoke. Stupid, stupid idea. You wouldn't catch Joan of Arc doing the Charleston. Forgive me, I don't know what came over me.

PERSEPHONE Yes well you're not a man. No well I mean you're not Reggie. And we've no music. Someone might see us. We'd mess up the floor. I mean I haven't got the right shoes. I don't need to dance that desperately.

DORA Yes all right, all right. It was stupid.

DORA starts cleaning vigorously.

PERSEPHONE I'm sorry about what I said earlier. You're not that bad.

DORA It doesn't matter.

Pause.

PERSEPHONE Oh damn it to hell. No come on. You're perfectly right. Dancing always makes me feel better. What's the worse that could happen? Someone will find us and think we're moral imbeciles. Which we are anyway. I'd love to dance, Miss Kitson. Thank you for asking me. Let's dance. We were born to dance.

DORA Well I wouldn't go quite that far.

PERSEPHONE I'll teach you the steps. No, wait, wait we must do this in style. Throw away our cleaning rags. Now picture this: I am wearing a full length shimmering silver halter-necked dress. My bosoms are just showing. I'm holding a long diamante cigarette holder. My hair is piled up and divine. I'm an actress. Adored by thousands. What about you?

DORA Well…

PERSEPHONE Come on, what regiment.

DORA Oh I see. Well maybe the 21st Lancers. Or I've always quite fancied the Green Jackets. At a push the Blues and Royals and if I could swing it, the Scots Dragoon Guards.

PERSEPHONE Who has the nicest uniform, Dora?

DORA Well the 21st's have splendid crushed velvet vermillion epaulettes.

PERSEPHONE Perfect. Perfect. Now I need an entrance. Hold on.

DORA I think you just set yourself alight with your diamante held cigarette.

PERSEPHONE Thank you for bringing that to my attention, Sergeant.

DORA Colonel. At the least.

PERSEPHONE Colonel then. Now you wait there. *(she is at the top of the steps)* Look the other way. Then spot me from afar.

DORA How can I do that if I'm facing the other way?

PERSEPHONE You sense me. Everyone has turned to look at me. Even the orchestra has stopped momentarily. Now, Dora, try it again. Remember I am the most ravishing creature you've ever seen. Everyone is hopelessly in love with me.

DORA I'm a soldier. I'm trained to keep my reactions in check.

PERSEPHONE Well just this once your guard has dropped. Now try it. *(DORA does)* Fine, fine. Now I'm making my entrance. Everyone is applauding.

(she comes down the steps) Now you approach me. Slowly and purposefully. Don't look down. You can't keep your eyes off me.

DORA Can I go back and try that bit again?

PERSEPHONE Very well. Now take my hand. Kiss it. *(DORA does so reluctantly)* Now ask me to dance.

DORA Excuse me, Miss Baker, would you care to dance?

PERSEPHONE Thank you kindly. Now put your arms around me. Not so stiff.

DORA It will be something slow and stately, won't it? Nothing too frantic.

PERSEPHONE Listen for the music, Dora. Oh yes. It's romantic. Now follow me.

DORA I should lead.

PERSEPHONE You don't know the steps. Look you'll pick it up and I'll pretend to follow… That's it. Not bad, Dora. That's it. Splendid. For a couple of imbeciles we really can trip the light fantastic. Oh yes, Dora. I'm there now. I'm almost there.

They dance. Music; Doris Day Move Over Darling

Scene Eight

PORPH You're such a good dancer, Dorph.

DORPH Thank you, so are you.

PORPH No I'm not.

DORPH Yes you are. You're very good at lots of things.

PORPH Like what?

DORPH I don't know. Well, air-swimming for one. You and me are the number one Great British synchronised air-swimming team.

PORPH I'm no good at anything. I'm stupid.

DORPH Don't say that, Porph.

PORPH Can I have a cat?

> **DORPH** *does not answer.*

> Sometimes I feel like nothing good will ever happen. It'll always be the same or worse.

DORPH Nothing is either good or bad but thinking makes it so.

PORPH Don't be clever.

DORPH Come on, smile.

PORPH I have never been one for artifice. It is a characteristic I despise. I am always exactly what I am. I always show exactly how I feel.

DORPH What are you talking about?

PORPH Doris said that.

DORPH I might have known.

PORPH Yes. If I am happy, I bloom with it, she said. And I'm exactly the same. And today I'm bloody miserable. I've got nothing to look forward to.

DORPH You never know what's round the corner. Your life is full of golden opportunity. Anything could happen.

PORPH Like what?

DORPH I don't know. Anything. You could meet the Queen. Eat oysters and champagne.

PORPH I prefer tea and crumpets.

DORPH All right, tea and crumpets and you'll wear white, you'll be a dream in white when you meet the Queen – satin and lace and voile and chiffon and gossamer and creamy calico.

PORPH I always look very drawn in white.

DORPH Porph you have to make things happen. You can't wait for them to come to you. What would you most like to happen?

PORPH I don't know. It's like I lost something really good along the way and I can't remember now what it was.

DORPH We'll get it back, Porph. We're the only ones who can make it happen.

PORPH Okay.

DORPH What's that, Porph? What's that?

> **DORPH** *goes to the box and gets out the hand whisk which she treats as a telephone.*

PORPH What?

DORPH I'm sure it's, yes I thought so it's the phone.

PORPH But –

DORPH Hold on, Porph. Yes, yes she is – it's for you.

PORPH I'm not in.

DORPH I'm sorry Porph can't get to the phone right now, can I take a message? Yes, yes, right, great. Yes I'll tell her. Okay thanks. Porph – you're going to have a baby.

PORPH What?

DORPH Yes, any day now. A little girl. A natural birth at home. The labour will be quite painful, but over quickly.

PORPH Who was it?

DORPH Oh Porph, I'm sorry. I didn't take their number. I could ring 1471.

PORPH No. I suppose it doesn't matter who it was, does it?

DORPH No, Porph.

PORPH A baby girl, you say? A sister for – …I'm glad the birth won't be too traumatic. You can be present if you wish. I'll keep the placenta. Yes I shall lightly grill the afterbirth and serve it with wild mushrooms and prosciutto ham.

DORPH I don't think that's strictly necessary, Porph.

PORPH It's very nutritious. What shall we call her?

DORPH Something noble. Like Artemis the Hunter.

PORPH Do you know I think I prefer Doris? My God, she's going to be pretty and sexy too, but only in moderation. Yes she must be pure. Pure as peaches. Oh and I shall love her, Dorph with such a big piece of my heart.

DORPH I know, Porph. I know you will.

PORPH I shall teach her to speak and walk and love and sing and dance and swim –

DORPH In the air, Porph.

PORPH In the air, Dorph and I shall feed her on satsumas and crispbreads.

DORPH That's a bit harsh, Porph.

PORPH She must be thin, Dorph. And she'll be mine. All mine and no-one will take her away from me.

DORPH No, Porph.

PORPH Are you sure?

DORPH Yes.

>   **PORPH** *is by now cradling her imaginary baby.*

PORPH But no Dorph, you see sometimes they come in the middle of the night, when you least expect them. You don't know who they are and they ask all sorts of questions. And everything depends on you getting the questions right. And sometimes you just can't get them right. And they say terrible things to you. Things to send you mad. And then you lose it, you see, Dorph. You lose the thing that was the most precious thing to you. And there's nothing you can do. Nothing...

DORPH It's all right, Porph. That won't happen anymore. I promise.

PORPH There's nothing you can do. There's nothing anyone can do. I've lost her, Porph. I've lost another one. I can't hug her into life. I just can't.

DORPH Yes you can. You're stronger now, Porph. You can hug her into life. This time it'll be all right. She'll be happy and healthy and American as apple pie.

PORPH Like Doris?

DORPH Just like Doris. Sing to her, Porph. Sing to your baby.

PORPH Yes. Oh she's crying, isn't she? She's so tired. She needs to sleep.

DORPH That's it, Porph. Sing her to sleep.

PORPH *(sings eight lines from* Secret Love*)*

During this.

DORPH Let's put her to bed now, Porph.

She takes the imaginary baby as **PORPH** *sings and puts her in the bath. We are back in the hospital.*

AIRSWIMMING

Scene Nine

PERSEPHONE I know I've been bad. But you can bring him back to me now. Please, please. I'll be good now. Just give him back to me now. Give him back. I demand that you give him back to me.

DORA What is it, Persephone?

PERSEPHONE They've done the most dreadful thing to me.

DORA What? Who? Who's done this?

PERSEPHONE I don't know. I don't know where he is. I put him down somewhere. *(she searches frantically)* Where's the water? You need plenty of hot water. He's here somewhere. Help me find him, Dora.

DORA Who is it? Who have you lost? Is it Reggie? Reggie's not here, Persephone. But it's all right. I'm here.

PERSEPHONE No, no. Stupid. Not Reggie. The little fish. My little toad. Where is he?

DORA I don't know.

PERSEPHONE Well, somebody must know. I'm going to the authorities.

DORA All right, now calmly, from the beginning. Where did you get the fish? Did you win him at the fair?

PERSEPHONE I don't know.

DORA Did Reggie give him to you?

PERSEPHONE He definitely had something to do with it. But perhaps it was Nana.

DORA Nana?

PERSEPHONE Only Nana would speak to me. She brought me my meals. I was in that nursery for months. Dirty, dirty girl. He was swimming around in my tummy. The little guppy. And then the pain. Phew Dora. I said, "Nana my tummy button hasn't opened yet". "Lots of hot water" she said. He was such a naughty little fish. But he was there all of a sudden. *(she laughs)* He jumped out like a salmon. Plop. The little slippery blue and red fish. Big brown eyes. He was the best thing I've ever had. Much nicer than that big hat. But then they took him away from me. They took him away.

DORA I'm sorry. I'm so sorry.

PERSEPHONE *(dawning realisation)* They brought me here because of the fish, didn't they? I shouldn't have had the fish at all. Only witches have fishes in their tummies. What a mess.

DORA Yes.

PERSEPHONE He was the only thing I ever had and they took him away from me. He didn't even have a name. I couldn't even give the bloody fish a name.

Pause.

DORA Come on we'll name him now. Hold him, Persephone, come on, hold him. *(she hands an imaginary baby to **PERSEPHONE**)*

PERSEPHONE But –

DORA That's right. Mind his head. We need some water. Wait there. Don't drop him. That's it. Right. By the power invested in me by…by…by St Dymphna, I baptise you… What? What do you want to call him?

PERSEPHONE What about Bastard?

DORA Persephone!

PERSEPHONE Well he was a bastard fish, wasn't he?

DORA We can't call him Bastard.

PERSEPHONE Why not?

DORA Well, it would ruin his chances with the army for one thing. No hope of Sandhurst with a name like that. Come on think, Persephone, what's he called?

PERSEPHONE I don't know. *(she looks hard into her arms)* Finlay. Yes, Finn. Finn, my little amphibian boy.

DORA *(with water)* I baptise you Finn in the name of the Father and of the Son and of the Holy Ghost… There Persephone. He's got a name. He's yours now. They can't take that away.

PERSEPHONE What can I do for him?

DORA Just love him. That's all any mother can do.

PERSEPHONE Oh yes I shall certainly do that. I would have liked to dress him in sailor suits. But never mind. What will be, will be. I'm tired now. Phew the pain of it, Dora.

DORA You sleep now. You deserve some rest. I can do the polishing today.

PERSEPHONE I want a big breakfast, I think. Eggs and crumpets.

DORA I'll see what I can do.

PERSEPHONE What year is it now, Dora?

DORA 1926.

PERSEPHONE Oh God. I've been here long enough now haven't I? How much longer will it be, Dora?

DORA I don't know.

PERSEPHONE Please tell me how much longer.

DORA The Great War lasted for four years.

PERSEPHONE Four years! What's great about that? But what about the Thirty Years' War, How long was that?

DORA It was longer.

PERSEPHONE Yes! And what about the Hundred Years' War. What about that? That went on for ever, didn't it?

DORA Yes, yes it did. There's no telling when it will stop. We have to put it out of our minds. We have to keep fighting. We're in this campaign together now. And we have to keep fighting.

PERSEPHONE Oh Dora, let's not think about it anymore.

DORA No, we'll start again tomorrow. Each day is a new day.

PERSEPHONE Thank you Dora. You're so strong, I was wrong about you. And about Reginald. I'd rather be in your regiment. I don't know what I'd do without this hour every day. Polishing. Ah well. Chin up. Good night, Dora.

DORA Good night.

Scene Ten

DORPH Porph, come here we need to practise some questions.

PORPH Why?

DORPH I've thought it over and we need to be prepared. In case someone comes.

PORPH But you promised me. You promised me I was safe. You said the dastardly man would never come. You said you'd protect me.

DORPH It's better to be prepared, Porph. That's all. I'm trying my best but I might not always be around.

PORPH But you promised!

DORPH I'm not as strong as you think. Sometimes you can't stop bad things happening. I'm just saying we should be prepared. Now come on. They'll be easy questions. You'll enjoy it.

PORPH Okay.

DORPH Right, let's see. What was Doris Day's real name?

PORPH She was born Doris Mary Ann von Kappelhoff to German Catholic parents in Ohio on 3rd April 1924.

DORPH Correct. What life threatening event happened to Doris at the age of fifteen?

PORPH She suffered a double compound fracture of her right leg when the car she was travelling in crashed into a train.

DORPH Correct.

PORPH I hope he doesn't ask me that. You know I get upset when I think about it.

DORPH We have to be prepared, Porph. Right. In which film did Doris star with Jimmy Cagney?

PORPH *Love me or Leave me.*

DORPH Correct. What was Doris's favourite film of the films she made?

PORPH *Calamity Jane.*

DORPH Correct. What was Doris's favourite pie?

PORPH Ah a trick question! Well most people assume it's apple when in fact of course, it's peach.

DORPH Is the right answer. You see you're very good at questions, Porph.

PORPH Well, I'm sorry Dorph but a five-year-old could get these questions right.

DORPH That's right, Porph, there's no need to be scared. Now how long have you known me?

PORPH For ever!

DORPH And have I ever upset you in that time?

PORPH You're my best friend, Dorph. What do you mean?

DORPH We're just practising questions, Porph. I've never hurt you, have I?

PORPH You won't let me have a cat.

DORPH No I mean, wicked hurt.

PORPH Of course not. I don't like these questions, Dorph.

DORPH No all right Porph. You must be strong. People say bad things about me. We have to tell the truth.

PORPH What things?

DORPH That I hurt people. I make people mad. That I made you mad. That I made your baby die.

PORPH No, no, no, no. I won't hear any more. You're getting confused. It was all such a long time ago. They don't know you. They don't know you like I know you.

DORPH We just have to tell the truth. That's all.

PORPH Yes, yes all right, Dorph. Now I've got a question for you. It's very hard.

DORPH Try me.

PORPH Why was Doris Day such a good actress?

DORPH Ah I know this one.

PORPH Come on then.

DORPH Because she was always confident, upbeat and absolutely sure of her destiny.

PORPH Like us?

DORPH No, Porph I don't really think so, do you?

PORPH No I didn't think so either. *(pause)* What do we do now?

DORPH Sit tight, Porph. We could be in for a long haul. So sit tight.

Time passes. Perhaps some music (Doris Day: Sentimental Journey*)? Stylized movement to show* **PERSEPHONE** *and* **DORA** *ageing in the hospital.*

Scene Eleven

DORA I think these stairs are clean don't you?

PERSEPHONE I can see my face in this bath.

DORA We've done a bloody good job, haven't we?

PERSEPHONE Well we've been doing it for a very long time, haven't we?

DORA And all this polishing has made me strong, you know. Arms like iron. I could swim the Channel, the Indian Ocean. When I get out they won't catch me for toffee. I'll join the Royal Irish Hussars. Fight the Hun. Do my bit... What is it?

PERSEPHONE My hair. My hair's grey. How terrible. When did this happen?

DORA Don't look.

PERSEPHONE I thought I looked better than this.

DORA You do.

PERSEPHONE My hair. My hair is –

DORA It's BROWN. Your hair is lovely and brown.

PERSEPHONE *(equally appalled)* Brown?

DORA Blonde then. Yes it's like spun gold.

PERSEPHONE Is it?

DORA Of course.

PERSEPHONE *(she decides to look away from bath)* Thank you, Dora. *(pause)* What year is it?

DORA Let's see. The date. Damn it. This isn't like me. 1930 something? 1940? It couldn't be, could it?

PERSEPHONE How long have we been here?

DORA Well I came in twenty two and you came in twenty four. How old am I? How old are you?

PERSEPHONE I forget. I was just about to come out then. So I must have been twenty one.

DORA Ten years? Twenty years? I don't know. It's not like me. I just don't know.

PERSEPHONE I wonder what we've missed. At any rate, it's got easier, hasn't it?

DORA In a way.

PERSEPHONE We must have missed things though.

DORA Don't look back. Don't look forward. Sit squarely in the centre of each moment.

PERSEPHONE You're much stronger than I am, Dora.

DORA No I'm not.

PERSEPHONE Oh yes you are.

DORA No the difference is I deserve this and you don't.

PERSEPHONE What rot. Never say that, Dora. Nobody deserves this.

Silence.

DORA My brothers all died.

PERSEPHONE I didn't know you had brothers.

DORA Three of them. In the war. All felled. Bang, bang, bang. So young.

PERSEPHONE I'm sorry, Dora.

DORA George was the eldest. Quiet chap. Very serious, academic, you know. Should never have been a soldier. Then Harry. The joker. Bit of a cad. You'd have liked him. But it's Alfred I think of most. Beautiful angelic boy with a mop of curls. Eighteen when he was killed. Eighteen. I should have done it. Fought the good fight.

PERSEPHONE You're a girl. A woman, Dora. You couldn't have done it.

Pause.

DORA Flora Sandes did it. In the Great War. She was a vicar's daughter. Captained a Serbian infantry unit against the Bulgarians. Brave as a bulldog. She was a vicar's daughter.

PERSEPHONE Well I'm very glad you weren't a soldier. Or a vicar's daughter for that matter.

DORA I should have done it though don't you see. Died for King and country.

PERSEPHONE No, Dora. No

DORA Instead of which this has been my National Service. The Royal Dymphonians. 1st Regiment. I've been a Dymphonian man and boy. Dymphonians are known for their stoicism. We're the backroom boys really – we're not the heroes, but we put in bloody years of service.

PERSEPHONE I think you're very brave. The bravest of the brave.

DORA Ha. An unsung hero. Perhaps I should award myself some medals. Decorations of valour. Polish them up. For another year's service. And another.

PERSEPHONE So you should.

DORA *(looks at* **PERSEPHONE***)* A bit of you thinks I'm mad. You do, don't you?

PERSEPHONE Dora!

DORA It's all right. I don't mind. But I mean the whole soldier thing. Come on I am a bit unhinged, aren't I? What was it? You hit the nail on the head once. 'A cigar smoking monomaniac transsexual?'

PERSEPHONE That was years ago. I did think so at first. But not anymore.

DORA I don't know how long I can keep it all up.

PERSEPHONE What?

DORA Active service, you know.

PERSEPHONE Dora, we've come this far. What do you mean?

DORA I want to retire. With a good pension.

PERSEPHONE Perhaps we will.

DORA No we won't... I'm not as sharp as I was. My fingers are all thumbs. I won't be able to change the fusillage. Won't be able to change it quick enough.

PERSEPHONE A minute ago you were going to swim the Indian Ocean.

DORA *(laughs)* Bravado, Persephone. Truth is I'm a coward. Always have been. That's why I fit in here. With all the other lost souls.

PERSEPHONE We're just tired. There's only so much polishing a person can do. It has got easier, Dora.

DORA Not for me.

PERSEPHONE I'll help you. You've always helped me in the past. It's my turn now.

DORA It's all right. I am fine really. Perhaps I will rest though. I wish I could remember what year it was. Yes just get my head down for a while. Lay low. I should know what year it is though.

PERSEPHONE That's the beauty of it. It can be any year we want.

DORA Not military doctrine but perhaps you're right. And I am exhausted you know. Always on my guard you see. In case they shave off my hair and find the Devil's mark.

PERSEPHONE Shh. Shush now. You rest. It's your turn to rest.

Scene Twelve

DORPH Where is it? Where is that bloody thing? She loses everything. Where the hell has she put it?

PORPH Dorph?

DORPH Ah you, yes. You. Where have you put it? Where is it? Come on where have you hidden it? Quickly. I haven't got all day.

PORPH What, Dorph? What? You're frightening me.

DORPH That bloody thing. Your bloody thingumy gadget. You know. Your fantastic labour saving device. I need to save my labour. So where the hell is it?

PORPH It's in the box.

DORPH Well come on then, get it. Come on I need it. You keep telling me how good it is. I need to try it.

PORPH Dorph, what is it?

DORPH Just get it. Give it to me. Quickly. Come on.

> **PORPH** *gets the hand whisk and gives it to* **DORPH** *who presses it to her head.*

That's no bloody good. Plug it in. Come on I need some power. It doesn't bloody work. Bloody typical. Bloody Moulinex.

PORPH No please, stop, Dorph. You're scaring me. I don't understand. What are you trying to do?

DORPH What does it bloody look like? I'm trepanning myself with a hand whisk. I'm trying to bloody well trepan myself with a sodding bloody hand whisk.

PORPH Please stop. Please, please, Dorph.

DORPH I can't even do this. God, give me strength. What are you doing? Are you completely thick? Turn on the power.

PORPH It's battery operated but I forgot to get any batteries.

DORPH I don't believe it.

PORPH You'll hurt yourself.

DORPH That's the idea.

PORPH No please, Dorph.

DORPH Don't you dare take it from me. Go away. I'm telling you for your own good. Go away. Leave me alone. Do you need me to spell it out for you? I don't want you here anymore. Do you hear me? Where's the book? Where's the bloody book?

PORPH What book?

DORPH The trepanning book, you idiot. Jesus Christ, where have you put it?

PORPH I didn't touch it.

DORPH You must have done. You touch everything. You can't keep your thieving hands off anything. Get out of my life, Porph. Go back to your family.

PORPH No, no, please, please stop.

DORPH I can't understand this. It won't work. It won't bloody work. I got the wrong bloody book. I should have got the bloody beginner's book.

PORPH What?

DORPH Trepanning for bloody beginners. For people who only want a small bit of happiness. That's all I want. A small bit of happiness. Nothing major. Just a bit of peace and quiet. On my own. What part of my head do I drill the holes in. I can't remember. Are you still here? BUGGER OFF. Go on, just sod off. I don't want you here anymore.

PORPH *is beside herself.*

Stop snivelling. You're a grown woman. You're not a child. God knows I've let you be a child for too long. You've got to grow up. Take some responsibility. Get a life! Leave me in peace.

PORPH I don't want to leave you.

DORPH Well I'll be leaving you soon enough whether you like it or not.

PORPH I won't let you go…

DORPH And how exactly are you going to stop me, Porph?

AIRSWIMMING

PORPH I'll take care of you. You won't be unhappy anymore.

DORPH You can't.

PORPH I can. I'll be like Doris Day in The *Thrill of It All* – you know when she plays Beverley Boyer and forsakes her own thriving career in soap commercials to look after her husband and children.

DORPH *(deadly)* Shut up about Doris Day.

PORPH But we love Doris.

DORPH No, Porph. YOU love Doris. I haven't even a passing interest in her. Do you know why? Because she's bland. She's completely fucking bland. I don't believe a word she says in her films. Her world doesn't exist. I can't bear her synthetic singing voice. And I hate blondes. I hate her in fact. In fact I would go as far as to say Doris Day has sodded my life up. She's completely sodded my life up.

PORPH But Doris wouldn't hurt anyone.

DORPH Oh no! You know what, Porph? Doris Day is a sham. A complete fabrication. A PR exercise.

PORPH No she's not.

DORPH And another thing you didn't know about Miss Perfect American Pie. She's a dyke, Porph. She didn't like Cary Grant. Oh no! She preferred Debbie Reynolds.

PORPH How can you say such things? I don't believe you. It's not true. That's disgusting.

DORPH Porph, it's staring you in the face.

PORPH No.

DORPH She was a plain, good old-fashioned carpet muncher, Porph. Take it or leave it.

PORPH Dorph, say you're sorry. Say you're sorry to Doris.

DORPH What?

PORPH You heard me. Say sorry to Doris.

DORPH She's not here.

PORPH She's always here.

DORPH No Porph, Doris Day is at this moment running a home for bewildered dogs on the other side of the Atlantic.

PORPH Yes, yes and as she loves animals so she loves us. So say sorry to her.

DORPH Grow up.

PORPH Since she isn't actually here, you can say sorry to me. In fact I have often been told there is an uncanny resemblance between myself and Doris Day.

DORPH No there isn't.

PORPH Yes there is I think you'll find.

DORPH No Porph. Let me tell you as your friend, that you are living a lie. You're not a bit like Doris Day. You're too short, you're too dumpy, you have no style and you look bloody ridiculous in that wig.

PORPH *(slowly takes off wig)* I hate you.

DORPH Good. That's a start. Pack your bags. Take your bloody whisk and go.

PORPH I won't. I won't leave you. You can say what you like. I'm not going anywhere.

DORPH Can't you see what you're doing to me? You're driving me mad. I can't cope with it anymore.

PORPH I'll help you.

DORPH Nobody can help me. I'm a lost cause. I'm not a very nice person, Porph. I'm not Doris Day. I'm wayward. I'm a witch. All my children are bastards. I have to be punished. I hurt people. I destroy things. They should lock me up and throw away the key. Just leave me to prepare myself. Find your family. Go back to them. You could still be happy. You've still got a chance.

Pause.

PORPH I think that was a little bit melodramatic, don't you? That's quite enough of that sort of behaviour. You just be quiet now, Dorph. It's my turn to do something for you. Come on Dorphy. You've always done everything for me.

DORPH You can't do anything for me.

PORPH I can wash your feet for a start. Have you seen the state of them? Cleanliness after Godliness, Dorph. There, sit there, give me your feet. Holy Dymphna, Dorph, they stink! There now just relax. You're very very tense, Dorph. Let me wash them. That feels better, doesn't it? (**PORPH** *washes* **DORPH** *'s feet*)

When I had my baby, I washed his feet. Tiny feet. So perfect. Like your feet.

DORPH Are you sure I haven't got six toes?

PORPH That's enough now. Just put it all out of your mind. There do you feel better?

DORPH Thank you, Porph I do. I just need to get some fresh air. I won't be long. But you must be on your guard. We have to be vigilant from now on.

PORPH I won't let you down, Dorphy.

DORPH Thank you Porph. I won't be long.

> **DORPH** *exits.* **PORPH** *sits on the steps. Possibly some music plays (Doris Day* When I Fall in Love*)? She tries to stay awake but gradually falls asleep.*

Scene Thirteen

DORA *enters and talks to the sleeping form.*

DORA Persephone. I know you're asleep. I don't want to wake you. I think it's time. Lay down my arms and all that. It's time to lie down and take it like a man. I don't know what year it is, you see, Persephone. I just don't know.

Pause.

I thought I was inviolable to attack. As stiff upper lip as my pater. I only wanted to wear men's clothes. Smoke a few cigars. A few shiny medals and a cricket box, you know the sort of thing. I thought we'd get out one day. Reward for years of service. We'd be handed it all on a silver platter. But the current's too strong, isn't it old girl ? My God, we've been treading water for years, haven't we? When we should have been swimming. Hades took us to the underworld, didn't he Persephone? But Demeter and the family just forgot about us. Forgot about us for years and years. How could they have done that? That's not how it was supposed to be. We were supposed to see the spring again, weren't we?

Oh listen to me rambling on. You're right, I do talk too much.

It's over now for me. You're still in with a chance. I did think you were a bit giddy at first but you're full of gristle, aren't you, Persephone? I've enjoyed our little chats. We've had a rum deal but we've made the most of it. I'll just go quietly. Don't want to make a song and dance of it. No need for the last post. Although the Victoria Cross might be nice. Awarded posthumously. Fix it for me, Persephone, would you? That would be nice.

She looks at her and leaves. **PERSEPHONE** *shifts in her sleep.*

PERSEPHONE Dora?

She goes back to sleep.

Scene Fourteen

DORPH *enters.*

DORPH Porph? Porph? Weren't you able to stay awake for even one hour?

DORPH *sits and looks at the sleeping* **PORPH**.

It's time, Porph. Be strong. Tell the truth.

Suddenly a light picks out **PORPH**. *She wakes up abruptly. During the next,* **DORPH** *fills the bath with water.*

PORPH Who is it? Whoever it is, go away.

DORPH You know who I am, Porph.

PORPH No I don't. Go away.

DORPH Come on, Porph. Don't be stupid.

PORPH I'm not stupid.

DORPH You know why I'm here, don't you?

PORPH *(unsure)* Yes.

DORPH How long has she been a witch, Porph?

PORPH I don't know who you're talking about.

DORPH Come on, Porph, don't mess me about.

PORPH I'm not.

DORPH I thought you were good at questions.

PORPH I am. I am.

DORPH You know what happens to bad girls. You don't want that to happen to you, do you now?

PORPH No. No I don't.

DORPH Why did she become a witch?

PORPH I don't, I don't know.

DORPH Porph, I'm losing my patience with you.

PORPH I know. I know.

DORPH Why did she become a witch?

PORPH Because she was always confident, upbeat and absolutely sure of her destiny.

DORPH Good girl. That's more like it. Who did she choose for her incubus, Porph?

PORPH Cary Grant. No. No. Debbie Reynolds.

DORPH Where did the Black Sabbath take place, Porph?

PORPH The Dorchester.

DORPH What music was played there and what dances did she dance?

PORPH Doris Day.

DORPH What dances, Porph. Come on.

PORPH We tripped the light fantastic.

DORPH What food did she eat there, Porph?

PORPH Eggs and crumpets, I think.

DORPH What animals did she bewitch to sickness and death?

PORPH My cat. No my little fish.

DORPH How can she fly through the air, Porph?

PORPH She swims. She swims through the air.

DORPH Has the Devil set a limit to her period of evil doing?

PORPH Any day now.

DORPH That's right, Porph. Good girl. No wait a minute. Were you her accomplice in evil?

PORPH Me?

DORPH Things are looking bad for you, Porph. Were you her accomplice?

PORPH No. Yes. No I –

DORPH But you do know her.

AIRSWIMMING 57

PORPH You see I –

DORPH You know her.

PORPH I'm not sure if –

DORPH You know her. She's your best friend, Porph. You must never leave her.

PORPH No. No. No I –

DORPH Are you lying to me, Porph?

PORPH No I swear that I don't know her. I'm telling you the truth. May God punish me if I'm not. I don't know her. I don't know her. I don't.

Lights fade up. **DORPH** *slowly lowers her head into the bath.* **PORPH** *scrambles to the top of the stairs. Then as if in slow motion,* **DORPH** *'ducks herself' three times into the water. Each time,* **PORPH** *goes to scream but although she can move her arms about and tear at her hair, no sound comes out of her mouth. The third time* **DORPH** *doesn't re-surface.* **PORPH** *is released.*

Dorph! Dorph! Dorph! Dorph swim. Dorph. Swim in the air, Dorph. Dorph. Please. Don't let this – Come on, Dorphy. Swim. Swim for Britain. Swim up Dorph. Swim up through the air. Dorph. Dorph. Dorph. *(trails off)*

Pause.

The dastardly man came, Dorph.

He asked me lots of questions.

I couldn't answer them, Dorph.

I'm in critical danger, Dorph. Do something.

Come on, let's sing. Sing ourselves to sleep.

Sings three lines from Que Sera Sera "Whatever Will Be, Will Be".

She falters.

I can't hug you into life, Dorph, I just can't. I can't make you mine. I've gone and lost the thing that was most precious to me. The game's up now, isn't it, Dorph? You'll never be happy and healthy and American as Apple Pie.

Sings seven lines from Bewitched.

Blackout.

Scene Fifteen

PERSEPHONE *is standing over the bath.*

PERSEPHONE Dora. Oh my God, Dora. Come on now. Don't do this to me. *(she lifts her out of the water and tries to revive her)* We're nearly there now, Dora. There's no need for all this. Come on Dora. Please, please Dora.

DORA *gasps for air.*

That's it. That's my girl. No, soldier. My brave little soldier. Come on, Dora. Come back to me.

DORA She died.

PERSEPHONE What?

DORA She died.

PERSEPHONE Who?

DORA Anne Dorphan.

PERSEPHONE Shush, it's all right. Calm yourself.

DORA In 1647 Anne Dorphan was drowned for being a witch.

PERSEPHONE Shush. Sshh. No more dates. I'm sick of dates.

DORA Do you know why, Persephone? For having more wit than her neighbours.

PERSEPHONE I know. I know. Oh you scared me Dora.

DORA Don't be clever, Dora. My father always said, don't be clever.

PERSEPHONE No, you must always, always be clever.

DORA I couldn't remember the year. Something snapped. And I couldn't remember the year.

PERSEPHONE It doesn't matter what year it is.

DORA I wanted to know though. I really wanted to know.

PERSEPHONE We'll find out. We'll find out. Hang on a minute. I saw a paper. They left us a paper for the polishing. Here it is.

She gets the paper out of the box.

DORA What's the year? Tell me the year. TELL ME THE YEAR.

PERSEPHONE 1958. *(reads)* Doris Day is voted the world's favourite actress by the Hollywood Press Association. There you go, Dora. There you go.

DORA *(pause)* Who's Doris Day?

PERSEPHONE I don't know – some actress.

DORA She must be good… 1958 you say?

PERSEPHONE Yes.

DORA And I came in 1922?

PERSEPHONE Yes.

DORA Thirty six years?

PERSEPHONE Yes.

DORA Thirty six years?

PERSEPHONE We can face it, Dora. We can face this. We've got the mettle. We can stare this in the face. But you mustn't leave me. You must never try this again. You're not leaving me now. Dora, I didn't ask to be put with you. But put with you I was and you're not taking the coward's way out.

DORA I was tired.

PERSEPHONE Being tired has nothing to do with it. Dora, you're a sergeant major. A bloody sergeant major. The Royal Fusiliers. In charge of. In charge of – help me out here Dora.

DORA Polishing?

PERSEPHONE Yes in charge of bloody damn well polishing. Guns at the ready. *(she wields her cleaning rag)*

Come on Dora. Caesar or nothing. Come on now.

DORA We're old now, Persephone. We're too old.

PERSEPHONE Well long live old people that's what I say. Vive la bloody France. What are the words to La Marseillaise? I want us to sing while we work. To hell with them. Come on, Dor, the Marseillese. Isn't that what Joan of Arc sang when she was being frazzled to a crisp?

AIRSWIMMING 61

DORA I don't think so.

PERSEPHONE Well she should have done the bloody frog. Come on Dora. Age cannot wither us.

DORA Nor polishing stale our infinite variety.

PERSEPHONE Absobloodylutely. Come on, Dora. Let's dance. We're the flappers. The original bona fide flapper girls. The limbs are slower but boy can we flap.

DORA I can't.

PERSEPHONE Of course you can. We're only just getting going. Let's kick up a stink. They made us mad when we were twenty and now we're young again. Let's dance for Caesar, for Joanie and for all the bloody nuts in here. Let's dance for us, Dora. Old witchy hags that we are. Come on.

DORA Persephone. I'll make a soldier of you yet.

PERSEPHONE Not bloody likely. Come on, Dor. Let's dance.

Music: Doris Day It Had To Be You.

They dance like two old ladies at a tea dance, supporting each other as they each in turn stumble and regain their balance.

Scene Sixteen

DORA What's the year, Persephone?

PERSEPHONE 1972.

DORA I thought so. Our Golden Jubilee. Well it's time. We're ready.

PERSEPHONE For what?

DORA To come out.

PERSEPHONE Where?

DORA To come out of here. They're letting us out.

PERSEPHONE We're coming out of Dymphna's? That's nice, isn't it?

DORA Yes, isn't it?

PERSEPHONE Do you want to do the bath or shall I?

DORA I fancy the stairs for a change.

They polish.

PERSEPHONE When will it be?

DORA Any day now.

PERSEPHONE At the Dorchester?

DORA No, no, just a quiet affair – no need for speeches.

PERSEPHONE No there's nothing to say really is there?

DORA No. They've arranged some council accommodation for us. Separate or together, whichever you prefer.

PERSEPHONE Oh together, I think if you don't mind. What will we wear?

DORA I think it has to be white, don't you?

PERSEPHONE Yes. Satin and lace and calico and butter muslin veils.

DORA And long, long gloves. There'll be food.

PERSEPHONE Champagne and oysters?

DORA No, tea and a battenburg.

They finish polishing.

PERSEPHONE I don't know if I can be bothered.

DORA No perhaps we should just stay in.

PERSEPHONE Yes I think it's raining. We could come out another day. *(pause)*

DORA You know, I think we'd better. If we don't now, we might never.

PERSEPHONE You're right.

They get ready to go.

DORA One thing.

PERSEPHONE Yes?

DORA Persephone is such a mouthful. I think I might call you Porph. In the next bit.

PERSEPHONE Very well. Then I shall call you Dorph.

DORA We'll be new people.

PERSEPHONE Anything's possible.

DORA We could grow pot plants and potter about.

PERSEPHONE And listen to nice music.

DORA It's quite exciting really.

PERSEPHONE Yes.

They stand uncertainly.

DORPH Are you ready, Porph?

PORPH Let's get cracking, Dorph.

DORPH Right.

Let's go.

They hold hands.

They swim through the air.

They repeat the same air-swimming routine although now they are much older and slower.

Lights fade.

Property List

Tin bath (p1)

Staircase or possibly a stepladder (p1)

A picture of a saint (St Dymphna) on the back wall (p1)

Polishing cloth (p1)

Bad Doris Day wig (p5)

Box (p15)

Book (p15)

Present – hand whisk (p17)

Goggles, swim caps and nose clips (p27)

Dorph fills the bath with water (p55)

Newspaper (p59)

Cleaning rag (p60)

Lighting

Lights up (p1)

Lights change, it is brighter, less hostile (p5)

Lights change (p10)

Suddenly a light picks out Porph (p55)

Lights fade up (p57)

Blackout (p58)

Lights fade (p64)

Sound

Music – Doris Day "Fly Me to the Moon" (p28)

Music – Doris Day – "Move Over Darling" (p34)

Perhaps some music – Doris Day "Sentimental Journey" (p44)

Perhaps some music – Doris Day "When I Fall in Love" (p53)

Music – Doris Day "It Had to Be You" (p61)

Ingram Content Group UK Ltd.
Milton Keynes UK
UKHW051256040523
421127UK00012B/153